AMAZING FISH

By Honor Head

Gareth Stevens
Publishing

Please visit our web site at www.garethstevens.com.
For a free catalog describing our list of high-quality books, call 1-800-542-2595 (USA)
or 1-800-387-3178 (Canada). Our fax: 1-877-542-2596

Library of Congress Cataloging-in-Publication Data
Head, Honor.
    Amazing fish / Honor Head.
      p. cm. — (Amazing life cycles)
    Includes index.
    ISBN-13: 978-0-8368-8895-9 (lib. bdg.)
    ISBN-10: 0-8368-8895-2 (lib. bdg.)
    1. Fishes—Juvenile literature. 2. Fishes—Life cycles—Juvenile
literature. I. Title.
    QL617.2.H43   2008
    596—dc22   2007043115

This North American edition first published in 2008 by
Gareth Stevens Publishing
A Weekly Reader® Company
1 Reader's Digest Road
Pleasantville, NY 10570-7000 USA

This U.S. edition copyright © 2008 by Gareth Stevens, Inc. Original edition copyright © 2007 by ticktock Media Ltd.
First published in Great Britain in 2007 by ticktock Media Ltd., Unit 2, Orchard Business Centre, North Farm Road,
Tunbridge Wells, Kent, TN2 3XF United Kingdom

ticktock Project Editor: Ruth Owen
ticktock Project Designer: Sara Greasley
With thanks to: Sally Morgan, Jean Coppendale, and Elizabeth Wiggans

Gareth Stevens Senior Editor: Brian Fitzgerald
Gareth Stevens Creative Director: Lisa Donovan
Gareth Stevens Graphic Designer: Alex Davis
With thanks to: Mark Sachner

Photo credits (t = top; b = bottom; c = center; l = left; r = right):
FLPA: 5b, 7t, 7b, 8 main, 11b, 12b, 16, 17, 20tl, 20c, 21, 25t, 27b, 28–29 main, 30c. JD Hill: 22tl. Nature Picture Library: 15cr,
15cl. NHPA: 14cl, 19b. Shutterstock: OFC, title page, contents page, 4tl, 4c, 5t, 6tl, 6b, 8tl, 9t, 9c, 9b, 10tl, 10 main, 11t, 12tl, 13t,
13b, 14tl, 14ct, 14cr, 14b, 15t, 15bl, 15br, 18 main, 19t, 23, 24tl, 24b, 25b, 26, 27t, 28tl, 29t, 30tl, 31t, 31 main, OBC. Superstock:
22c. ticktock image archive: map page 6, 18tl.

Every effort has been made to trace copyright holders, and we apologize in advance for any omissions. We would be
pleased to insert the appropriate acknowledgments in any subsequent edition of this publication.

Printed in the United States of America

1 2 3 4 5 6 7 8 9 10 09 08 07

Contents

Words in the glossary appear in **bold type** the first time they are used in the text.

Scales help
protect fish from
underwater dangers.

What Is a Fish?

A fish is a **vertebrate** that lives in water.
Vertebrates have backbones. Fish breathe
underwater using openings in their bodies
called **gills**. The gills take **oxygen** from the
water and pass it into the fish's body.

Fish usually have fins and
scales. Fish use their fins
and their tail to move
through the water.

Fin

Gill cover

Fin

Some fish live alone. Others live in big
groups called schools. A school can have
hundreds or even thousands of fish.

A female fish attached these eggs to an underwater rock.

Most fish reproduce by laying eggs. The eggs are very small and soft. Female fish usually lays hundreds of eggs at a time.

Sharks are a type of fish. Some sharks, such as the great white shark, give birth to live babies called pups.

The great white shark is one of the most feared fish in the ocean.

Tail

AMAZING FISH FACT
Great white shark pups are more than 3 feet (1 meter) long at birth. They have sharp teeth and are ready for hunting!

Fish Habitats

Blue tang fish live in holes and cracks on coral reefs.

A **habitat** is the place where a plant or an animal lives. The ocean is a habitat, and so are rivers and lakes. Many fish live in the ocean, which is salt water. Other types of fish live in freshwater ponds or streams.

Fish live in all the world's saltwater oceans. They also live in most of Earth's freshwater lakes, rivers, ponds, and streams.

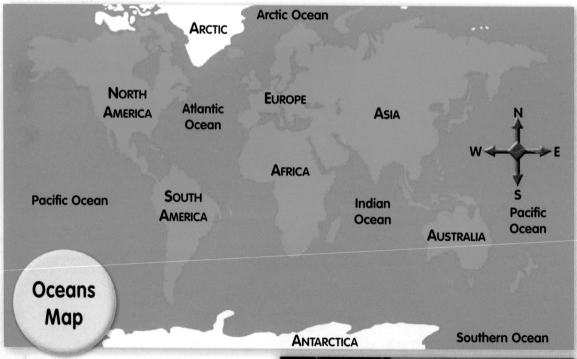

Arctic Ocean

ARCTIC

NORTH AMERICA

Atlantic Ocean

EUROPE

ASIA

N

W E

AFRICA

S

Pacific Ocean

SOUTH AMERICA

Indian Ocean

Pacific Ocean

AUSTRALIA

Oceans Map

ANTARCTICA

Southern Ocean

Some of the most colorful fish in the ocean live around **coral reefs**. These reefs grow near the surface in warm-water oceans.

The Pacific and Indian oceans have many coral reefs.

Some strange-looking fish live deep in the ocean. The deep ocean is cold and dark. Very little food can be found there.

The fangtooth lives deep in the ocean. It is easy to see how the fish got its name. The fangtooth sinks its thin, sharp teeth into its **prey** so it won't get away.

The mudskipper is a fish that lives in shallow water in muddy freshwater **swamps**. It spends most of its time out of water and can "walk" on its fins.

Fin

Ocean Fish

Ocean fish can be just a few inches long or huge, like the whale shark—the biggest fish in the world! Some ocean fish look more like seaweed or stones than fish.

Stonefish live on the ocean floor. They look just like stones and have a nasty sting!

Whale shark

AMAZING FISH FACT
A whale shark can grow to nearly 50 feet (15 m) long. It's not a hunter, though. It mainly eats **plankton**.

The leafy sea dragon lives in warm oceans around Australia. It hides in seaweed, using its leaf-like decorations as **camouflage.**

Many fish that live in coral reefs have bright colors or patterns that help keep them safe from **predators.**

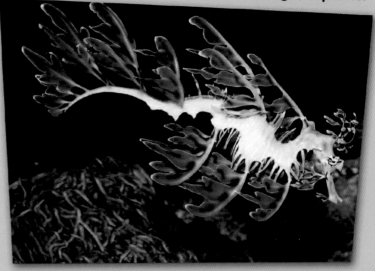

A leafy sea dragon is hard to spot among sea plants.

Pretend eye

The butterfly fish's black spot looks like an eye. A predator is not sure which end is the right end to attack.

Sea anemone

Clown fish

The clown fish hides from predators among the stinging tentacles of **sea anemones.**

The clown fish's body is covered with a special slime. Scientists believe the slime protects the fish from the anemones' stings.

Freshwater Fish

Perch live in rivers and lakes. Females lay up to 300,000 eggs at one time!

Some freshwater fish live in clear, flowing streams or rivers. Others live in ponds where the water is very still and where lots of weeds grow.

Catfish live in lakes and rivers. They eat fish, shellfish, and any other small creatures they can find. Catfish usually feed at night.

AMAZING FISH FACT
Catfish use their long whiskers, or barbels, to feel for food along the bottom of lakes and rivers.

Barbel →

Piranhas live in freshwater rivers in South America.

Piranhas eat other fish, insects, seeds, and fruit. Sometimes piranhas eat larger animals!

If the river dries up during a hot time of year, the piranhas are forced to live together in a small amount of water. If a large animal, such as a horse, steps into the water, the hungry piranhas will attack as a group!

Piranhas have razor-sharp teeth.

Mom Meets Dad

Male and female long-nosed butterfly fish pair for life.

Most fish reproduce every year. Some fish find a partner and stay together as a pair for life. Other fish find a new partner each year. Many fish **mate** with more than one partner in the same year.

Hammerhead sharks can live in schools of more than 500 sharks. The strongest female swims in the middle of the school.

When she is ready to mate, she starts shaking her head from side to side. This signals the other females to swim to the edges of the school. The strongest female is then the center of attention and sure to get a mate!

AMAZING FISH FACT
Sharks live in all the world's oceans. They have been around since before the dinosaurs!

Freshwater angelfish stay together as a pair for life. After mating, the female lays about 1,000 eggs on a leaf and waits for them to **hatch.**

Eggs

A pair of angelfish guard their eggs.

A male emperor angelfish lives with up to five female mates. Sometimes female fish develop into males. If the emperor angelfish male dies, one of the females turns into a male fish and becomes the leader of the group!

Emperor angelfish live on coral reefs.

What Is a Life Cycle?

A **life cycle** is the different stages that an animal or a plant goes through in its life. The diagrams on these pages show the usual life cycles of most fish.

This is a pair of red flower horn fish. There are about 24,500 different types of fish.

THE LIFE CYCLE OF A FISH

A pair of lionfish

1 An adult male and female fish meet. Some fish make a nest.

Fertilized fish eggs

2 The female fish lays eggs. Then the male fertilizes the eggs.

A pair of angelfish

3 Some fish guard their eggs. Others leave them to hatch on their own.

Baby salmon

4 Baby fish called fry hatch from the eggs. The tiny babies take care of themselves. They have a yolk sac that they use as food.

THE LIFE CYCLE OF A SHARK

A pair of nurse sharks

1

An adult male and female shark meet and mate.

A blacktip shark pup

A female lemon shark and pups

3

As soon as they are born, the pups take care of themselves. They have teeth and are ready to hunt.

2

The female shark gives birth to several pups at one time.

Sea horse

Lionfish

Amazing Fish Life Cycles

In the pages that follow, we will learn about the life cycles of some amazing fish—from tiny sea horses to colorful lionfish.

The female anglerfish can open
her mouth wide enough to eat
fish that are bigger than she is.

Deep-Sea Anglerfish

Deep-sea anglerfish live in the darkest depths of the ocean. The female has a long fishing lure built right into her head. The lure has a light on the end to attract prey.

Food is hard to find in the deep sea. The light on the anglerfish's lure is always "on." That increases the fish's chances of finding a meal.

Light

Lure

Male anglerfish are much smaller than the females. Some types of male anglerfish cannot catch their own food. They attach themselves to a female.

The male anglerfish becomes part of the female's body! When she eats, the food goes into the male's body, too.

Female

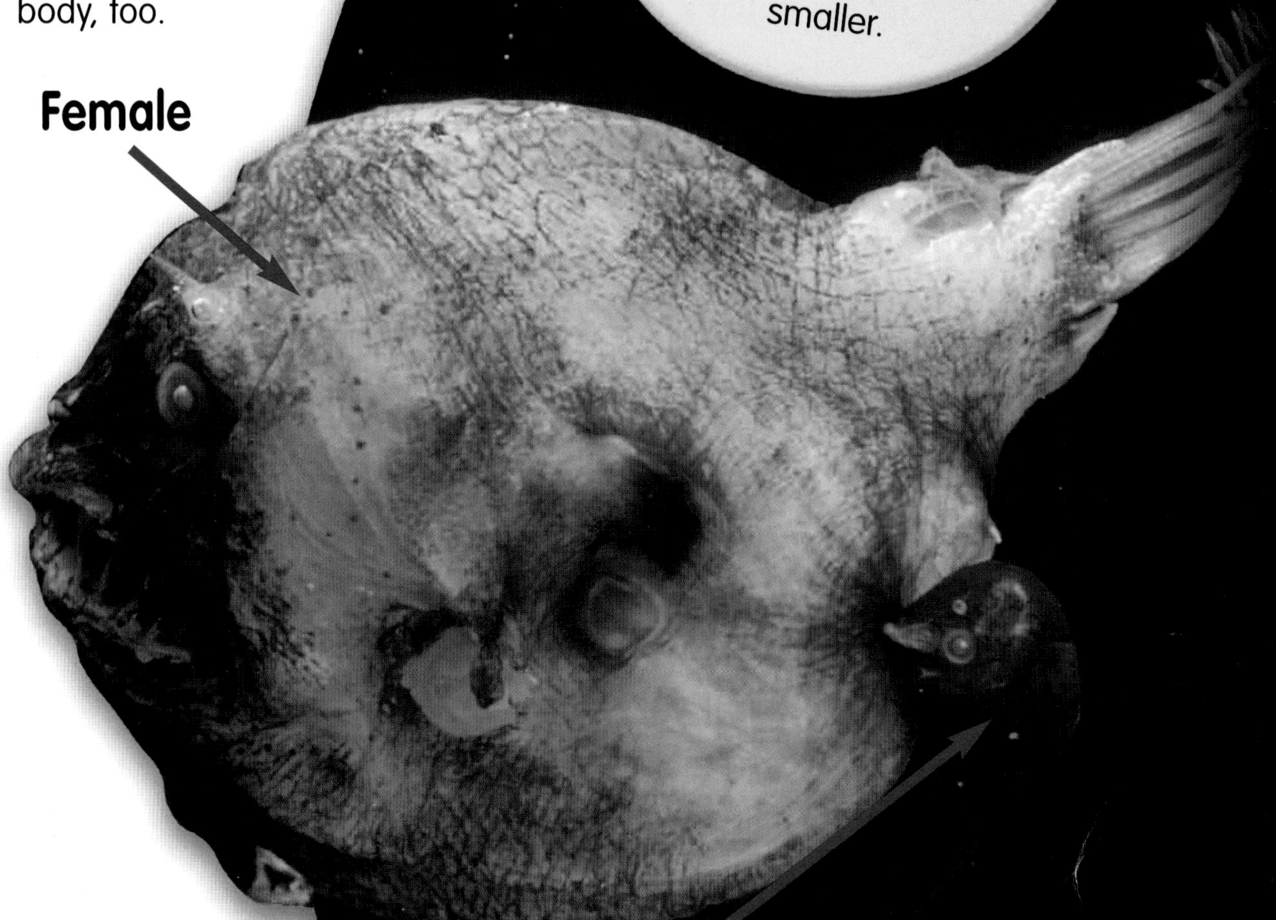

When it is time for the female to reproduce and lay eggs, she already has her mate with her!

Male

A salmon that is ready to
reproduce is called a spawner.

Salmon

Adult salmon live in the ocean. In the autumn, they return to the river or stream where they were born. There they mate and die. Their babies will one day make the same long journey.

The salmons' trip is sometimes thousands of miles long. They must swim **upstream**, which is very tiring.

**AMAZING
FISH FACT**
Salmon must leap up waterfalls and avoid predators, such as grizzly bears.

Grizzly bears

Salmon

When a female salmon reaches the place where she was born, she makes four or five nests called redds. She lays about 1,000 eggs in each nest. A male fertilizes the eggs.

Thousands of spawners gather in the same place.

The eggs hatch after four months. Salmon fry are called alevins. They have an orange yolk sac that contains all the food they will need to grow.

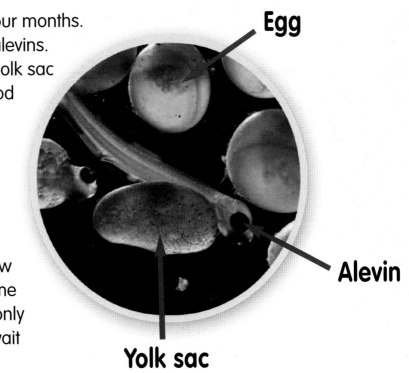

Egg

Alevin

Yolk sac

The young salmon grow bigger and bigger. Some swim out to sea after only a few weeks. Others wait up to three years.

Sticklebacks feed on tiny shellfish and the eggs of other fish.

Stickleback

Sticklebacks are tiny fish. They grow to just 2 inches (5 centimeters) long. Some sticklebacks live in salt water close to the coast. Others live in freshwater ponds, lakes, or rivers.

Between March and August, the male stickleback changes color to attract a mate.

Nest

The male stickleback builds a nest from small pieces of plants. He does a zigzag dance in front of the nest to attract females.

During mating season, the underside of the male's body becomes a bright orange-red color. His eyes turn blue, and silver scales appear on his back.

Many different females lay their eggs in the male's nest. The male then fertilizes the eggs.

Male

Female

Dogfish

Dogfish are a type of small shark. Adult dogfish are about 3 feet (1 m) long. They spend most of their time on the seafloor, hunting for crabs, shrimp, and small fish.

Like all sharks, dogfish have skeletons made of cartilage. This is the bendy material in your ears and your nose.

After mating, the female dogfish lays her eggs. Each egg is in its own little leathery case.

Lesser-spotted dogfish are found along the mud and gravel of the seafloor.

The female attaches the egg cases to pieces of seaweed so they do not float away. The baby dogfish growing inside the case is called an **embryo**.

The embryo will stay in the case for about nine months. As it grows, it curls around the inside of its egg case.

The egg cases are full of food for the embryos to eat.

By the time the baby dogfish is ready to hatch, it is about 4 inches (10 cm) long. That's twice as long as its egg case.

AMAZING FISH FACT
Empty dogfish egg cases sometimes wash up onto beaches. Some people call them mermaids' purses.

Egg case

Embryo

23

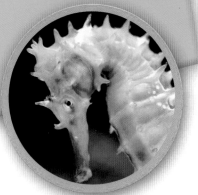

The sea horse's body is covered by armor made of hard, bony sections.

Sea Horse

The sea horse has a horse-like head and a tail it can use to hold on to things. The sea horse can move each of its eyes separately. One eye can look forward while the other looks backward.

Before they mate, male and female sea horses may hold each other's tail. They may also swim side by side or swing together on a piece of seaweed.

Most types of sea horses pair for life.

The male sea horse has a pouch on his belly. The pouch is like a pocket. The female lays her eggs inside the pouch, and the male carries the eggs.

When the babies are ready to hatch, the male holds on to a piece of seaweed with his long tail. He rocks backward and forward until the babies pop out of his pouch. This is a lot like giving birth!

Pouch

Baby sea horses

AMAZING FISH FACT
Sea horses can change color to match their surroundings.

**Lionfish live on coral
reefs in warm seas.**

Lionfish

Adult lionfish usually live alone.
When they are ready to mate, they
get together in groups. For three or
four days, each male tries to get a
female to notice him.

Sometimes the males fight. They
bite each other and ram each
other with their spiky fins.

**AMAZING
FISH FACT**

The lionfish's needle-like
fins can give predators
a poisonous sting.

Fins

Adult lionfish are about 12 inches (30 cm) long.

When the male has found a partner, the two fish swim face-to-face and turn around in circles. They "dance" like this up toward the surface of the water.

Near the surface, the female lays a ball of thousands of eggs. When the male has fertilized the eggs, the parents leave. The eggs hatch after about three months.

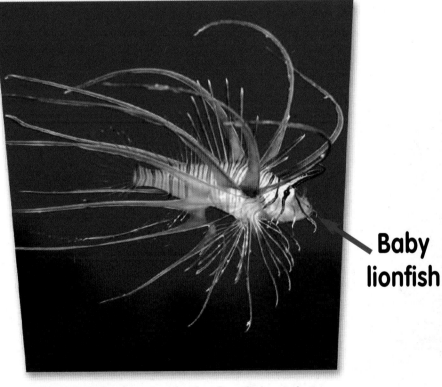

Baby lionfish

After hatching, the baby lionfish sink to the seabed to hide from predators.

The largest hammerhead is about 20 feet (6 m) long.

Hammerhead Shark

Hammerhead sharks live in warm areas of the Pacific, Indian, and Atlantic oceans. They are strong swimmers and have been known to attack people!

Dorsal fin

The hammerhead has an eye at either end of its wide head. Scientists believe this might help the shark see all around it when it is hunting.

Gill slits

Stingray

Hammerhead sharks eat other sharks and fish. Stingrays are their favorite food.

Eye

AMAZING FISH FACT

Some sharks have several rows of very sharp teeth. When a tooth falls out, one from the row behind pushes forward to take its place.

The female hammerhead shark gives birth to 20 to 40 pups at a time.

The pups are about 28 inches (70 cm) long when they are born. They look like small versions of the adults. The pups have to take care of themselves as soon as they are born.

Many of the pictures in this book were taken with a special underwater camera.

That's Amazing!

All fish, big or small, use their gills to breathe underwater. Humans breathe through lungs. Photographers must wear special diving suits and breathe from an oxygen tank to take photos of all the wonderful fish in the sea.

The ocean sunfish can grow to 10 feet (3 m) in length. It is not a threat to divers.

AMAZING FISH FACT
Unlike most other fish, the ocean sunfish does not have a tail.

A female sunfish can lay 300 million eggs each year. Each egg is smaller than the period at the end of this sentence.

Some fish, such as the flounder, are flat. But they are not born flat. When they are young, they have a round body with an eye on each side.

Eye

As the flatfish grows, its body becomes thin and flat. One eye moves across the top of the fish's head until it is next to the other eye.

Manta rays are huge plankton-eating fish. They swim by flapping their fins the way a bird flaps its wings.

The female manta ray gives birth to one or two babies each year.

The ray's fins can measure 23 feet (7 m) across.

Diver

31

Glossary

camouflage: colors, marks, or a shape that hides an animal from predators and its prey

coral reefs: underwater structures made from the skeletons of tiny sea animals called coral polyps (PAH-lips)

embryo: the first stage of development for an animal or a plant

gills: breathing organs in fish and other animals that live in water

habitat: the natural conditions in which a plant or an animal lives

hatch: to break out of an egg

life cycle: the series of changes that an animal or a plant goes through in its life

mate: to come together to make eggs or babies

oxygen: a gas that all animals need to stay alive

plankton: tiny animals and plants that live in oceans and lakes

predators: animals that hunt and kill other animals for food

prey: animals that are hunted by other animals as food

scales: hard plates of skin that cover the bodies of fish and reptiles

sea anemones: poisonous ocean animals that look like a plant

swamps: very wet areas with many water plants

upstream: the direction opposite to the flow of water in a river or stream

vertebrate: an animal that has a backbone

Index